Ladybird Picture Books

Indoor Things

Outdoor Things

Things That Go

Things to Wear

Things to Play With

LADYBIRD BOOKS, INC.
Auburn, Maine 04210 U.S.A.
© LADYBIRD BOOKS LTD MCMLXXXVIII
Loughborough, Leicestershire, England

Printed in England

Outdoor Things

Illustrated by **Ethel Gold**

Ladybird Books

red

weather vane

barn

stop sign

fire hydrant

orange

hose

lawn mower

barbecue

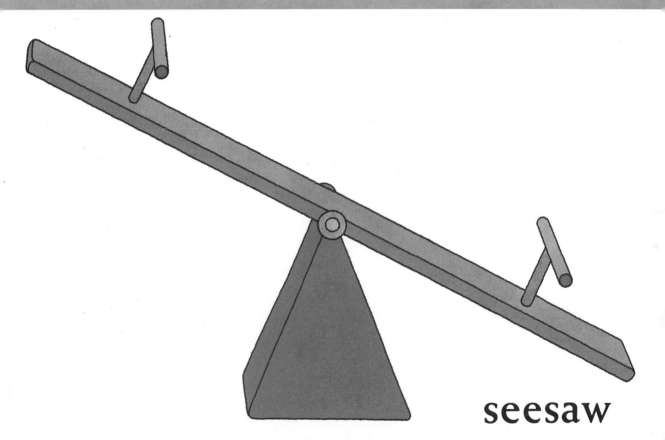

seesaw

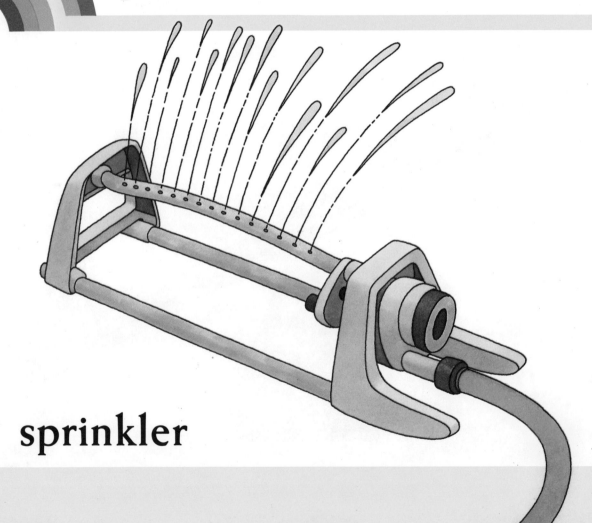

yellow

sprinkler

flowers

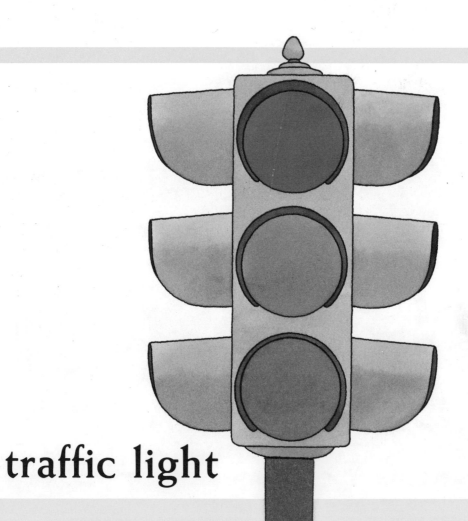

traffic light

swing set

green

bench

tree

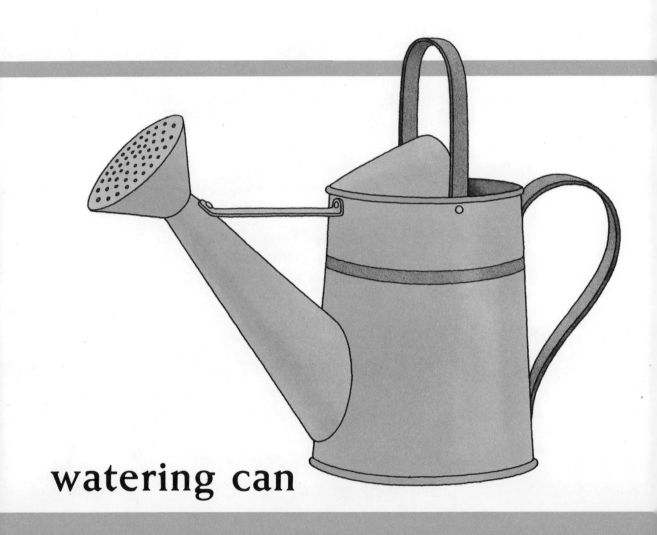

watering can

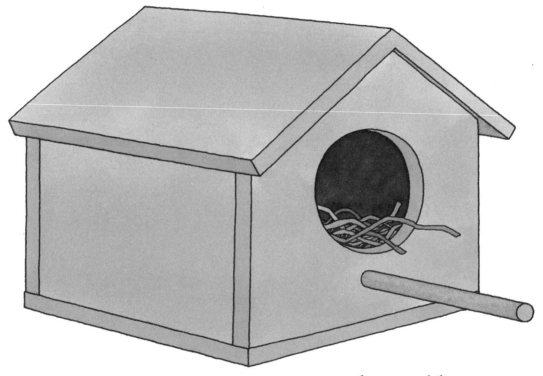

birdhouse

blue

streetlamp

mailbox

trash can

shovel

purple

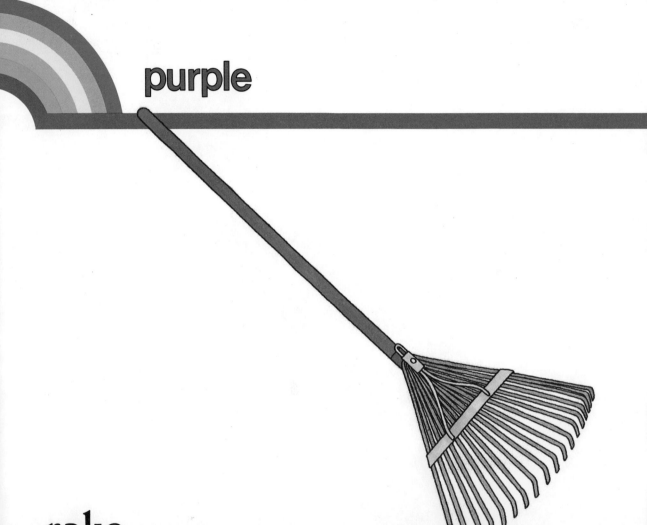

rake

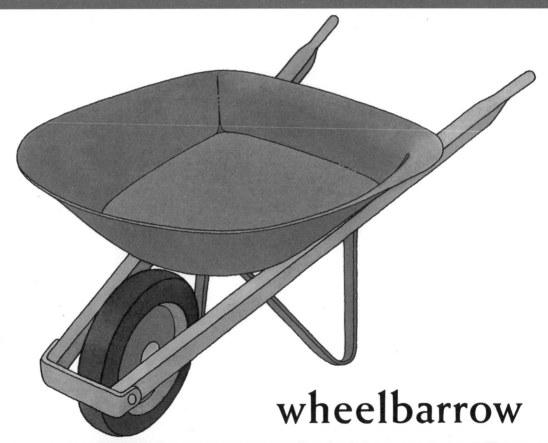

wheelbarrow

jungle gym

umbrella